THEN AND THERE SERIES

GENERAL EDITOR:
MARJORIE REEVES, M.A., Ph.D.

The Norman Conquest

MARJORIE REEVES

Illustrations drawn from contemporary sources by

H. SCHWARZ

LONGMAN

LONGMAN GROUP LIMITED
Longman House
Burnt Mill, Harlow, Essex. U.K.

First published 1959
Fourteenth impression 1981

ISBN 0 582 20378 3

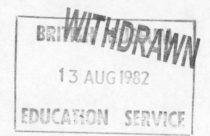

Printed in Hong Kong by
Sheck Wah Tong Printing Press Ltd

CONTENTS

The illustration on page 55 is reproduced
by courtesy of the Public Record Office.

TO THE READER

ENGLAND has not often been conquered, but once at least she was invaded and beaten all in a few weeks. Who were these Normans who conquered England, and how did they manage to do it? Many people can tell you that William the Norman won the Battle of Hastings in 1066, but they do not know what really happened there and how William conquered and governed England after the battle. To answer these questions we have to read the *chronicles*[1] written while men still remembered what had happened and we have also to study a famous set of needlework pictures, called the BAYEUX TAPESTRY, which was made soon after 1066. In this book I have tried to tell you what the chroniclers said and to show you many of the pictures. It is always exciting to discover what really happened and I hope you will enjoy trying to find out about this famous battle and famous conqueror in English history.

Here sits Harold, King of the English

[1] You will find the meaning of words written like *this* in the Glossary on pages 59–60.

THE COMET

IT WAS the 24th of April in the year 1066. All over England that night little groups of men stood outside their homes pointing at the sky.

Some of them shrieked and all shivered and crept into their beds cold with fear. For what they saw was a great fiery star with streaming fiery hair that blazed through the inky-blue sky. We should call it a comet and learned astronomers in our newspapers would tell us a great deal about it. People in 1066 also called it a comet, but they did not know what it was and so they were afraid. Men whispered that it was a sign of dreadful troubles that were going to happen in England.

Here you can see some men pointing at and discussing the comet. One of them runs to tell Harold.

People were expecting trouble in April, 1066. A few months before, King Edward had died suddenly. He had been a gentle, holy king—that is why we call him Edward the Confessor—and all men mourned for him. But the great question was: Who would be king in his place? Edward had no son to succeed him and everyone feared that there would be fierce fighting for the Crown. So, very quietly, on the very day of Edward's funeral, Harold, the son of Godwin, had been chosen as king. He was a splendid leader in battle and so men hoped he would save England from wars.

But away on the other side of the English Channel, in the part of France called Normandy, there was another great fighter who meant to have England. This man was William the Norman.

England and Normandy

HAROLD AND WILLIAM

William pretended that the Crown of England was really his by right. He said that Edward the Confessor had promised it to him. He also told a strange story about Harold. He said that about two years before Harold had been ship-wrecked on the coast of France and would have been killed if William had not rescued him. Harold, said William, had then promised to help make William king of England when Edward was dead. Here is a picture which the Normans made to show that the promise (or *oath*) which Harold took was a very solemn one. Harold is touching with his finger some very holy things while he is making the promise:

Harold made an oath to Duke William

William was angry when he heard that Harold had broken his oath and had got himself crowned king. He called a council of all his chief men (they were called *barons*). After a good deal of arguing, he persuaded them to sail with him across the sea on an expedition to conquer England. As a bribe he promised them rich lands in England. Then he sent messengers round the neighbouring lands offering rewards to everyone who would come and fight for him. All the most warlike men came crowding in, eager for the adventure.

William began at once to build ships, to gather together horses and food, and to pile up bows and spears. There was a great deal of work to be done before he was ready to invade England.

Here are some of his men chopping down trees as fast as they can.

They wanted
the timber
to build
ships.
Here they
are building
the ships.

The work was done in all haste, and as soon as possible William's men were dragging the boats to the sea. Notice the fierce animal heads they have carved on the *prows*.

hIC TRAhVNT:NAVES:ADMARE

Here they drag the ships to the sea

5

Here the men are carrying armour to the ships. Can you see the coats of *chain-mail* (called *hauberks*)? They are so heavy that two men have to carry each one on a pole. There are swords, spears, and a battle-axe as well, while several men carry helmets:

These men carry arms to the ships

What was Harold doing all this time? Just what you would expect. He was gathering the largest army ever seen in England. His spies slipped across the Channel in little boats and hurried back to tell him about William's army and navy. But this was not Harold's only trouble. In early summer his bad brother and great enemy, Earl Tostig, came across the seas with many ships. He raided the Isle of Wight, burning and robbing, and then sailed along the coast to Sandwich and so up to the Humber, doing damage everywhere. Wherever Harold tried to catch him he slipped away. Poor King Harold did not know which way to turn! Every day he expected news that William the Norman and his army were sailing across the Channel. If he turned his back on them and went north to chase Tostig there would be no one to stop the Normans landing. So all through the summer Harold kept his army and fleet at the Isle of Wight and along the south coast, watching for William's ships. But the weeks went by and no William appeared. When it came to the 8th day of September the men in the army had eaten up all their provisions and would not wait any longer. So they all began to go home and Harold gave up the watch for William.

Then suddenly terrible news came Another Harold—King of Norway —had come by surprise with a large navy to Tynemouth in the north and Earl Tostig had joined him.

On this map you can see the positions of all Harold's enemies.

The North Sea

7

Harold, King of England, dashed away north, riding night and day and trying to collect an army as he went. On September 24th he came to Tadcaster and heard that Tostig and the other Harold were in York. So on Monday, September 25th, he rode hard for York and clattered right through the city in chase of his enemies. He caught them by surprise and at Stamford Bridge a great battle was fought all day. At the end of it Harold, King of Norway, and Earl Tostig lay dead and very many men with them, both Norwegians and English. The rest of the Norwegians fled to their ships. Harold, King of England, was victor.

But what had William the Norman been doing all the summer with his army and navy all ready. Why had he not sailed for England? All his ships were ready, all the food and drink on board, all the soldiers assembed at the sea-port of St. Valery at the mouth of the river Somme, but day after day the wind blew the wrong way! You see, these were not steamships but sailing ships that needed a following wind to billow out their sails. If you look again at the map on p. 7, you can work out for yourself what kind of a wind they were waiting for. North, south, east or west wind?

William's men got impatient waiting and—as idle people so often do—began to get into mischief. But William was very firm with them. He forbade them to quarrel or fight with each other or ride away on adventures of their own. He would not let them steal eggs or poultry or meat, or trample on the corn, or do any other damage to the country folks' property. He gave them all enough to eat and kept them ready to board their ships at the first breath of the right wind.

THE GREAT INVASION

At last the right wind blew—but it was not until the 27th September. Then there was such a hurrying and scurrying to board the ships with all possible speed. Knights snatched up their helmets and bridled their horses, men called for their companions as they ran and would not stop for anyone, so eager were they not to be left behind. The Duke rode up and down spurring on the slow ones and urging all to make haste.

Many years after this great day, some ladies worked for many days and put the whole exciting story (as the fighters in the battle had told it to them) into pictures which they embroidered in a long strip called the Bayeux Tapestry. We still have this tapestry today. The pictures you have already seen in this book are taken from it. So now we will follow the story right through using the pictures the Norman ladies made. Remember that they found battle scenes difficult to draw and work in needlework—you would too, I expect—and so some of their pictures are rather curious. On each picture they embroidered Latin words to show what was happening. You can find out what these words mean by turning to page 56.

Now was the time when Harold should have been on the shore with all his army! When men are anchoring their boats and wading ashore it is easy to attack and beat them. But where was Harold? The Battle of Stamford Bridge had been fought on the 25th September. It was now the 28th September, but Harold was still up north at York, about 250 miles away. There were no telephones or radio in those days, of course, so Harold only got news of William's landing when a messenger galloped night and day to tell him. How long do you think that rider took?

While the messenger was galloping north William's army had all landed on the beach. Here they are riding to the town of Hastings to get food. Notice that they have put on their heavy *hauberks* as a safeguard, but they do not need their helmets yet because there is no fighting.

You can see them killing animals and carrying off meat.

The food in the ships had long since been eaten and everyone must have been very hungry, for here they are cooking and eating a good square meal. Notice how the cooking is done and how small birds are served on the skewers on which they had been roasted.

Here the servants serve

Here they have dinner

Here Duke William is sitting with his two half-brothers on either side of him. One is Odo, Bishop of Bayeux; the other is Robert, Count of Mortain.

They were two of his chief advisers. Perhaps they are telling him in this picture that it would be good to make a fortified camp or castle at Hastings, in case of sudden attack.

In the next picture you see the men bringing spades, digging the moat and throwing up the mound for the castle. The *keep* on top was put up very hastily and only made of wood for the time being. Can you see two men who seem to be hitting each other with their spades?

(William) orders a castle to be dug at Hastings

One day a messenger rode up to William to tell him that Harold had won a great victory over the King of Norway and his brother Tostig at Stamford Bridge and

14

that even now he was hurrying south to fight William. Here the messenger is giving the news. Don't you think William looks rather scared? He had been waiting at Hastings for some days, wondering where Harold was and how big an army he had. Now he was really coming!

Harold was very anxious too. He had rushed his army up north and fought and won a big battle. Now they were rushing south again as fast as they could. They were stout-hearted men but very tired. Many foot soldiers had been left behind because Harold rode so fast. He had sent messengers around the country-side to collect reinforcements, but they had not yet arrived. However, Harold did not stop for them; on he galloped until he came near Hastings.

Here a messenger from William met Harold. He solemnly declared that William was the rightful King of England and that Harold had broken his promise to William. He said that if Harold would not submit, King William would rather fight him alone than have the two armies kill each other. But Harold refused. "We march to battle", he said. "May the Lord decide this day between William and me, which of us has the right".

THE BATTLE OF HASTINGS

Here is one of William's knights all ready dressed in his *hauberk* and just going to mount his horse.

And here is a band of Norman knights riding out to battle from Hastings.

And they advance to battle against Harold the King.

16

Here William is making a speech to his army, telling them to be brave.

He said: "There is no road for retreat. In front the enemy blocks the way; behind there is the sea with an enemy fleet waiting for you. But do not be dismayed. The English are not famed as fighters. Only be bold so that nothing shall make you yield and victory will gladden your hearts".

Here are the Norman knights with their spears tilted, ready for the signal to gallop forward.

You will notice that in front of the mounted knights are archers. This was part of William's plan. Harold had dismounted all his men and placed them in close formation on top of a hill near an old grey apple-tree. At the sound of a trumpet-blast William's archers let off a thick cloud of arrows and instantly his knights galloped forward up the hill behind the arrow-attack.

Here you can see them advancing. Notice how Harold's men stand so close that their shields make a shield wall to protect them. Harold had commanded them to stand close like this and on no account to break their ranks. Can you see the Norman arrows sticking in their shields?

The English have chosen their position well, right on top of the hill. If only they could stand firm and never let the shield-wall break, they might win! Again and again the Normans charged up the slope at them but the English hurled back spears and *javelins* or chopped at them with battle-axes.

Both sides were so fierce in attack that soon many men, both Normans and English, and many horses, too, were falling to the ground.

At one moment there was a dreadful rumour that William was dead. This made some of his men lose courage and begin to run away. But William thrust himself in front of them, pulled up his helmet and shouted: "Look at me well! I am still alive and by God's grace I shall yet be victor. What is this madness that makes you flee?"

In this picture you see William showing his face at this moment.

19

So William stopped the flight of his men and again they hurled themselves on the English wall of shields. Yet the English were still unbeaten so long as they kept in their close mass. At last, however, the Normans hit on a trick and pretended to run away, tempting many English to leave their close ranks and pursue them. Then the Normans turned on the English and cut them down. So the strong shield wall on the hill was broken. Here you see a Norman knight attacking a few who are left on the hill.

Now the Normans began to win. Here you see the English fighting valiantly but falling before the Normans.

And now the last disaster befell the English: King Harold was killed! In this picture you see him twice over —first pulling an arrow out of his eye and then falling in front of a Norman knight on horseback.

Harold had been brave and gallant and tireless. He had fought two great battles and ridden hundreds of miles in a few days. Now he was dead, and now at last the English lost heart and fled.

WILLIAM IS KING

Harold was dead, but William did not know what the English would do next, so he went back to Hastings and waited for five days. Can you imagine the dismay of all the English as their soldiers rode home through the country with the news of the great defeat? Should they fight again? Many were wounded and weary and had no heart for another battle. Beside, who would lead them now? There were two great earls named Edwin and Morcar who planned to make Prince Edgar, a cousin of Edward the Confessor, king in Harold's place. They met with several other English leaders in London and there they argued with each other as to what they should do. But no one trusted the others and all were afraid of William. So the days slipped by and no great leader arose to put courage into the English and lead them once more against the invaders.

William waited for the English people to submit to him, but when no one came he decided to show people what a wonderful and fearful conqueror he was. So he marched to Dover and the men of Dover—although they had a wonderful strong castle high on a rock by the sea, were so filled with fear as they saw the Norman army approaching that they gave in at once. Then William burnt the castle and all men trembled. From Dover he went towards Canterbury and the men of Canterbury came out to meet him in order to prevent their city being burnt. So he went on towards London and everywhere frightened men submitted to him

William's route

As William approached the south bank of the Thames, Englishmen, fleeing in front of him, approached London Bridge and told the people in the City how William's men were plundering and burning the villages through Kent. The City was packed with soldiers and people who had come in for safety. Stigand, the Archbishop of Canterbury, was there, and so were Aldred, Archbishop of York, and the earls Edwin and Morcar, and Prince Edgar. They argued long with the chief citizens of London: should they go out to fight or should they submit? Some were for fighting and when they saw the advance-guard of William's Normans just across the river, a small band dashed over London Bridge to fight them, but were driven back inside London's walls.

23

But William did not attack London Bridge. Instead he marched westwards along the south bank of the Thames. He went west until he was miles from London and had reached the ford and bridge at Wallingford. There he crossed the river easily without any English army to stop him, and turned back towards London. Look at the map on page 23 to trace out the way he took. You can think out for yourselves why he took such a roundabout route.

The English soldiers might have crossed London Bridge and come up behind him to fight, but they never got up enough courage. Perhaps the rich merchants of London prevented them from fighting, for fear of losing their wealth. Anyway, by the time William had circled round and was slowly marching back towards them, their courage was gone. At Berkhamsted a miserable little band of men met William: there were Archbishop Aldred and other bishops, the earls Edwin and Morcar, Prince Edgar and many chief citizens of London. They came to surrender the keys of the City to William. So London, the most important town in England, was conquered and William's worst trouble was over. Had the Londoners been firm in fighting, William might have found England far more difficult to conquer, but because they could not agree, London fell and with it most of England was William's.

When the Normans rode through the streets a few rash Londoners still tried to fight them, but most stood sullenly and let them pass. William himself waited outside London for some time. He wanted to be crowned King of England in the proper way and this meant that he had to be properly chosen by the great council of the English called the *Witan*. In this way he hoped to make himself the true successor to Edward the Confessor. The Witan, including the two archbishops and the earls Edwin and Morcar, gave up the idea of making Prince Edgar king, and agreed to choose William. So at last, on Christmas Day, 1066, William rode solemnly through the streets of London to Westminster Abbey, the beautiful new church built by Edward the Confessor, where he was crowned King of England. It was the second coronation to take place in Westminster Abbey: the first one had been only a few months before. Since then the coronation of every King or Queen of England has been held in Westminster Abbey. Inside the Abbey the chief men in the Witan and many other Englishmen were assembled and all the chief Normans as well. The Archbishop of York made a speech to the English. He said that England must have a king and that God had sent them William, Duke of Normandy. Then he asked them if they would have William as their king and all the English shouted with one voice that they would. After this a Norman bishop, Geoffrey of Coutances, made a speech to the Normans, asking if they, too, would have William as king and they also shouted for him. Next, Aldred made William promise in a solemn Coronation Oath to rule England as well as the best kings before him. Finally, he set the royal crown on William's head and led him to the throne. So Duke William of Normandy became King William I of England.

Outside the Abbey—alas—a sad thing happened while all this was going on inside. There were crowds of Norman soldiers waiting there as well as crowds of English. When the Normans heard all the shouting inside they thought William was being murdered, so, in a fury, they started to kill the English and to burn their houses. Before they could be stopped many people were dead.

25

THE ENGLISH REBEL

If you had been William, what would you have done next? Though he had captured London and been crowned King of England, he did not know whether the English would rebel against him in some other part of England. Remember that he and his Normans had no maps of England such as we have, so that they really did not know what they had conquered. Remember, finally, that William had bribed his Norman barons to come with him by promising them rich lands. Now they were eagerly waiting for their rewards and some threatened to go home at once if they did not immediately receive all that William had promised them. One story even says that their wives, away back in Normandy, began to make a fuss and sent messengers to tell them to come home at once!

So William had to act quickly. After a quick visit to Normandy to talk to the wives and other people, he started at once to march through various parts of England. Everywhere he went he gave the lands of the rebel English to his Norman barons and ordered them to build castles as quickly as possible. The first castle to be built, however, was to make London safe for the Normans, and that was the great, grim stone Tower of London.

Many other parts have been added to this castle since William's day, but you can still see the *keep* built by the Normans. They built it to frighten the Londoners, for, although they had elected him king, William did not trust them to stay loyal. You can imagine how the Londoners would look up fearfully at its great, thick walls, knowing

that if they angered King William his knights would
quickly ride out of "the Tower" to burn their houses and
perhaps kill them.

The Keep of the Tower of London, built by the Normans

William's first march was down to the south-west of England. There Harold's family, the House of Godwin, still had many friends, and the city of Exeter was threatening to fight for Harold's sons. But the sons had fled to Ireland and the Exeter men who started to fight when William appeared outside their walls, were soon beaten. William did not punish the men of Exeter very severely but he ordered them to start at once building one of the strong Norman castles. Soon they were groaning away, digging out the moat, throwing up the great earth mound and dragging up stones to build the keep on top.

On his next expedition from London, William marched north, first to Warwick, where he ordered a castle to be built and gave great lands to Robert de Beaumont who had fought bravely at Hastings. The Beaumonts held these lands for the king many years and, although much has been added to it, you can still visit at Warwick the castle they built. Then William moved on to Nottingham where he had another castle built and made William Peveril keeper of it. Finally he marched to York where two castles were built, one on each side of the river.

As William shared out the lands of the Englishmen among his Norman barons, many more castles were built up and down England. Find out if there was a Norman castle anywhere near where you live. Who built it? The Normans preferred to choose the top of a hill or a high rock or cliff for their castles, but if the ground was flat then they piled up a great mound of earth (which they called a *motte*). It was the English who had to do the hard work of digging and hauling timber or great blocks of stone to the top of the mound. At first, because they were in a hurry, the Normans often built a wooden keep on top of the mound (as they had done at Hastings), but gradually these were replaced by strong stone keeps that could defy any attack. This picture is a good example.

Rochester Castle

When the king ordered a castle to be built in a town, the Normans cared nothing about people's houses. Down they came if they were in the way, and the poor folk had no choice but to rebuild their homes somewhere else. In Lincoln 166 houses were destroyed to build the castle, in Cambridge 27, and so it was in Oxford and many other towns. The English groaned in misery but few had the strength to fight back.

So William scattered his tough, hard-fighting Norman barons in various parts of England. He put one half-brother, Bishop Odo of Bayeux, in Kent, and another, Count Robert of Mortain, in Devon and Cornwall. Later on, he gave Shropshire to the energetic Roger Mont-gomery, with Shrewsbury castle for a centre, and sent Count Alan of Brittany to Yorkshire. Soon these and many more barons were riding through England with their own bands of knights, exploring their new lands and forcing the English to obey them. As they clattered on their horses through the villages the English looked at them with fear and hatred, wondering what these new rulers would do to them.

Have you ever seen a fire start in the dry grass? A few sparks fly—and in an instant it is blazing in half a dozen places. "As dry as tinder, just waiting for the spark," we say, and two years after the Conquest England was like the dry grass—just waiting for a few sparks to blaze out in rebellion. The sparks came. In the south-west the sons of Harold came sailing across from Ireland to the coast of Devon and Somerset. Westwards, in Shropshire and Cheshire, a fierce fighter called Edric the Wild rode round the country rousing people against their Norman masters. Up in the north angry men sharpened their swords and spears against the Normans. A sudden quarrel was the signal for a rebellion in which they killed Robert Cumin, one of William's earls. Soon after this, Danish friends appeared off the coast in their ships, eager to join in the fight against the Normans, and together the English and Danes captured York, driving the Normans out.

William and his barons might well have lost their nerve, with rebellion blazing up all round them. But they stood firm and acted quickly. In the south-west some English actually helped the Norman side, and the sons of Harold were quickly driven back to their ships. Edric the Wild was defeated by William himself near Stafford, and then the king turned north, determined to punish with terrible severity the men of the north country who were the toughest rebels. The Danes fled and the Normans recaptured York, but this was not enough for King William. When it suited him he could be mild with people, but now he was very angry. Slowly he marched through Yorkshire: every village he came to he ordered to be burnt, all the sheep and cattle killed, all the food destroyed. It was winter. Can you picture the bewildered folk suddenly homeless in the bleak weather? Many of them had never thought of rebelling against William, but now they froze and starved as they wandered through the bare land that William had laid waste or *harried*, as men said. Even some of the Normans were shocked. They thought that God would punish William for his cruelty. Years later a monk in Normandy, named Orderic Vitalis, wrote about William's harrying of the north:

Never before did William commit so much cruelty. He set no bounds to his fury, but ordered corn, cattle and every sort of food to be collected in heaps and set on fire. Innocent children, young men and old died of hunger. Undoubtedly such *ferocity* did not go unpunished by God, the all-powerful judge. I have praised William often but I dare not praise him for a deed which brought all, good and bad, to one ruin.

When the terrible harrying was finished William led his army right over the Pennine hills in the midst of winter. Even now people sometimes get stuck in the snow high on the top, and you can imagine what it was like in those days when there were no proper roads.

William's knights grumbled, but they feared the king more than the hills, and somehow he forced them on through the snow and over the heights until they came down into Cheshire, where they caught some of the last rebels. So Cheshire was conquered and after a while William gave it to a strong earl named Hugh Lupus, or Hugh the Wolf, who was very fat but very fierce.

Now William and his barons had crushed all the rebels in the south-west and midlands, in the north and north-west. But there was still one stronghold left, where the last English tried to hold out against William. In eastern England there are the Fens. The country here is flat and through it wind many streams and rivers.

In those days you could look for miles and see nothing but swamps and rushes or marshy lakes with islands.

Today, much of the water has been drained away and safe roads have been made, but in William's day it was a dangerous place for those who did not know the secret tracks through the swamps, for you could easily be sucked in and drowned.

In the midst of the Fens is the island of Ely, now no longer a real island but then surrounded by waterways and marshes. Here the last of the English rebels gathered together. We know some of their names. There were Siward Bearn, Bishop Egelwine, Earl Morcar and many hundred *thegns* and *peasants*. (Edwin and Morcar had been at William's court, you remember, but they had fled away and wandered aimlessly in the forests until Edwin was killed and Morcar came to Ely.) There were famous fighters and stout-hearted men in Ely, but the most famous of them all was Hereward the Wake. In later years men told tales of his mighty deeds—how he could fell the stoutest man with his fists, how he could fight half a dozen men at once with the sword he called Brainbiter, how he had a horse called Swallow which was swifter than any other. These stories are not all true, but when Hereward and his men clattered down the road, shouting "A Wake! A Wake!", William's Normans probably preferred to keep out of the way. Now the last chance of the English had come and in Ely they worked furiously, barricading the island with wooden fortifications, while in the famous old abbey English monks prayed for their success.

When William heard what they did, he came against them with boats and a great army. But it was hard to cross the swamps. The legend of Hereward tells how William ordered a *causeway* to be built over the bog, but it was not strong enough. When William's men crowded on to it in

33

their heavy armour, the causeway sank. Then the swamp was full of Normans who were slowly smothered in the black mud. William swore a great oath and came back again with another army. This time he built a stronger causeway and had many boats, but the story says that while the army was crossing Hereward set fire to the broad beds of dry reed on either side of the causeway, so that a great fire swept right over and destroyed many men. But at last, so says the story, the monks of Ely got frightened and let in William's army while Hereward was away searching for food. Many of the brave English were killed, but Hereward probably escaped. William admired a brave man and perhaps deliberately let him go. We do not know for certain what happened to him. But in Northamptonshire there still lives today a family named Wake who say they are descended from Hereward, the last unconquered Englishman.

NORMANS AND ENGLISH SETTLE
DOWN TOGETHER

Now at last William could feel that he had really conquered England. The sons of Harold never came back
again; Edwin and Morcar were dead. Only one English
earl, Waltheof, still had any power. He was loyal to
William for several years but then two of the King's
barons who were discontented persuaded him to join
them in a rebellion. They were all beaten and poor
Waltheof was executed. William tried to keep Prince
Edgar at his court so that he could do no harm, but soon,
in fear and hatred of the Normans, he fled secretly to
Scotland with his sister Margaret. They found a home in
the court of King Malcolm of Scotland, who married
the good and beautiful Margaret. With them went many
of the English thegns: England was no longer safe for
them and they refused to live under the hated Normans.

Other thegns sought adventure in many parts of Europe.
Some went to Scandinavia where they fought and sailed
the seas with the Vikings. Some went as far as Constanti-
nople, the famous capital of the Eastern Emperor, where
they enlisted in his finest regiment, called the Varangian
Guard, and fought bravely in many battles far away in
Asia. So some had strange adventures and saw gorgeous
palaces, but many of the English were quiet men who
only wanted to stay at home and farm their own lands.
They accepted William as their king and tried to settle
down, but they found life very hard. Only a few were lucky
enough to keep all their lands. Many lost a great deal and

most of them found they had new Norman masters put over them. There was one man named Ailric of Marsh Gibbon who, we are told, used to hold his land freely in the time of King Edward but now, in King William's time, held it from William, son of Ansculf, for rent, heavily and miserably. Many more groaned in the same way.

To the poor countryfolk, perhaps, the Norman Conquest did not make so much difference. They had always worked hard for English masters, and now they worked for Normans—though probably harder. But they were more tied down, less free and more harshly punished. The English groaned under Norman rule and said that God had sent William as a punishment for men's sins.

Sometimes they did more than groan, for fierce anger would flare up when a Norman master was particularly hard or cruel. Then the English would watch for a chance to catch him unawares. Perhaps he would go hunting and stray away from his companions alone into the deep forest. Then the English peasants, slipping silently through the trees, would shoot him with bow and arrow and vanish as silently as they came, leaving the dead body to be found by his Norman friends. So many Normans were murdered in this way that William had to make a new law saying that if the murderer was not to be found, the whole district in which the dead body of the Norman had been discovered must pay a heavy fine.

Yet, strangely enough, the English people did not really want William to go away. Many of them thought that one strong king was better than several leaders all fighting to be king, and William, as you have seen, was strong enough to keep even his great Norman barons in order. He would not let them grab just anyone's land as they pleased, but insisted that they should take just what he gave them and no more. He would say, "You shall have the lands of Leofric the Englishman" or some other English thegn who had fought against William. But before the Norman could receive his land the king made him take two solemn promises of loyalty and service which were called an oath of *homage* and an oath of *fealty*. First the Norman baron knelt in front of the king, put his hands between William's and said something like this:

> I promise to become your man, to hold these lands faithfully and perform my due service, preserving your earthly honour in all things.

The King would reply:

> I take you to be my man.

Then the baron would stand up, place his hand on the Bible and take the oath of fealty:

> This you hear, my lord, that I will bear you fealty with my life and limbs, body and *chattels* and earthly honour. So help me, God and these Holy Gosepls.

So the baron became William's man or *vassal*, as he was called.

In the picture on the next page someone who saw a vassal doing homage has tried, not very successfully, to draw it. You see the king sitting on a seat, but the artist has drawn the vassal standing up, perhaps because he could not draw him kneeling down! The plants are meant for corn to show the lands he is going to receive.

So William would grant the baron his *fief* (that is, his lands), and tell him exactly what services he had to do

37

A curious picture of a vassal doing homage

for the king in return for his fief. William might command him to bring ten or twenty or fifty knights to the kings army whenever the king summoned him, or he might tell him to send knights for guard duty at one of the great new Norman castles, or he might order him to do something special, like carrying the king's standard to battle. Whatever his particular service was, the Norman baron, who had now become one of the king's *tenants-in-chief*, must be sure to do it punctually, coming with his proper number of knights, fully armed and ready, whenever the king called him.

When the new tenant-in-chief went to his lands he probably took his own band of knights with him. Sometimes, to make sure of having the full number ready when the king summoned him, he would divide up some of the lands the king had granted him and give them to his own knights, making each responsible for some of the service he owed to the king. These knights (who were called *sub-tenants*) would swear homage and fealty to their lord, just as he had done to the king. Each would promise to provide one or two or five or more knights for the king's army. But the Norman baron generally kept a good deal of the land for himself and sometimes he kept it all. Then he would have his knights close round him, living in his castle and eating in his own hall. It was useful to have them so near, in case of sudden attack, especially if he lived on the Welsh border. The Welsh at this time were wild and fierce and William placed strong Norman barons along the Welsh borders, who built stout castles, like this one, and garrisoned them with good knights.

Ludlow Castle

39

These knights were trained to fight on horseback. In peace-time they practised with their horses and rode against each other in mock fights. Their weapons and armour had always to be kept polished and ready. When the king's messengers came galloping through villages and towns to summon the army, or *feudal host*, all the knights who owed *feudal service* must be ready to ride forth at once. First they would join their own lords and then, all over England, you might have seen bands of armoured horsemen—twenty, thirty or more in each—winding through muddy lanes or trotting along the old Roman roads, all going to one place—the spot which the king had commanded for the *muster* of his feudal host.

When they were all on parade, with the sunlight gleaming on spear and helmet, William must have thought he had a splendid army. But he was not quite sure how far he could trust them. Suppose one of his great Norman barons rebelled—would his knights fight for their lord or for the king? William decided to try and make sure that the most important knights belonging to his barons were loyal to him, so he summoned to Salisbury all his barons and the chief sub-tenants. On the wide grassy downs near Salisbury all these men gathered and there William made them all take a solemn oath to serve him first, before any other lord. This is how a monk described the Oath of Salisbury:

> There his councillors came to him and all the people owning land who were of any account over all England, whosoever's vassal they might be, and all bowed down to him and became his men and swore oaths of fealty to him that they would be loyal to him against all other men.

William kept a tight hand on his Normans. In the law-courts he tried to see that the English had fair play. He would send a letter to his officer (called the *sheriff*) rather like this one:

> 'See that this Atsor the Englishman has his land of Edingdale honourably for the service by which his father held it, and see that no man does him wrong therein."

Even though the Norman sheriff himself might be the man who was keeping Atsor out of Edingdale, he would not dare to disobey the King's letter.

When there were disputes about land, he often trusted what the English said against the Normans. Once in a big dispute he ordered a very old English bishop to be taken in a cart all the way to court so that he could say who had the best right to the land. William made some new laws and expected both Normans and English to obey them, but he also commanded that the old English law of Edward the Confessor should be kept. By and by, when the English had settled down a little, many of them began to feel that William, though stern, was their safeguard against the Norman barons. So, when two Norman barons got tired of William's stern law and rebelled against him, a surprising thing happened—the English fought for William and helped him beat the rebels.

Two people who saw clearly that one stern master who made people keep the law was better than twenty lawless ones, were bishops. One was Aldred, Archbishop of York, who, you remember, crowned William in Westminster Abbey. The other was Wulfstan, Bishop of Worcester, a very holy man who loved all the stories of old English saints and kings, yet worked loyally for William as the new king, and even rode to battle for him when the Normans rebelled. William wanted good bishops in the

Church, so, as soon as he could, he brought from Normandy a great man named Lanfranc, to be Archbishop of Canterbury in place of Stigand. William and Lanfranc worked hard together for the good of the whole Church. They brought over keen men from Normandy to be bishops and abbots in England and they built many new cathedrals and churches, almost as strong and thick-walled as the castles. Just as the castle-builders did not hesitate to destroy people's homes, so, if the church-builders found a little old English church in the way, down it came. Many of these old churches were small and no doubt the Normans thought the new ones would be grander, but it was a sad thing that they were destroyed. In some places you can still find bits of old English churches—and a few whole churches escaped.

Anglo-Saxon church at Bradford-on-Avon

At Bradford-on-Avon in Wiltshire the Normans left the little stone church on one side, close to the new, big one. It stood for centuries, forgotten or used as a cottage, until, not so long ago, someone suddenly discovered it was the first church. See if you can discover in your neighbourhood any remains of old English churches. Find out the Norman churches, too: you can recognise them by their thick, round pillars and round-headed arches and windows, as in this picture.

Stewkeley Church

43

Lanfranc and his Norman bishops were rather scornful of the English Church. They thought there were too many saints, and yet they admired the chief English saints like Cuthbert of Durham and Aldhelm of Malmesbury. They thought the priests were very badly educated and tried to start new schools to teach them. They did not like the way the old bishops used to journey round the countryside on foot with the bishop's staff in hand, like shepherds looking after their sheep. They thought bishops ought to be good business-men and live in the midst of busy towns. So, many of the bishops moved their houses from small villages to important cities like Winchester and Lincoln. They became important people, living grandly with many servants and working hard for King and Church, but perhaps some of the English sighed for the simple, saintly men who once walked through the villages, preaching to the people.

Peterborough Cathedral

44

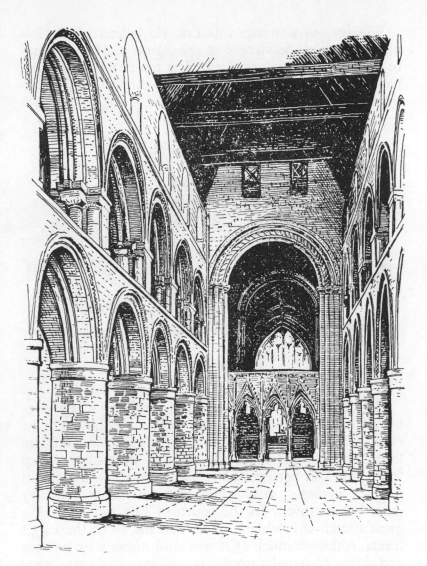

Southwell Cathedral

William was a strange mixture. He believed that God had given him the victory at the Battle of Hastings and to show his thankfulness he built a monastery where the battle had been fought and called it Battle Abbey. Here is a picture of it.

Battle Abbey

He prayed devoutly, did good to the Church, and protected priests and monks from harm. Yet he could be cruel and harsh when he wanted his own way. William loved hunting and especially the red deer in the deep forest. He was determined to have good hunting and if peoples' homes or crops interfered with his sport, they must be destroyed. In the south of England he took a great stretch of heathland and woodland to be the king's forest. Although much of it was wild, there were villages and farms scattered through it and many of these were wiped out. It was terrible to see the king's men going

46

through, turning out the peasants and burning their houses, all for the king's pleasure. Today we still call it the New Forest. Here and in many other forests William chased the red deer and the wild boar. His son, William Rufus, was also a keen hunter. Perhaps you already know the story of how he was killed by an arrow when hunting in the New Forest.

Here you can see the king's dog just about to pull down a deer.

Not all the countryfolk in the king's forests were driven away, but anyone who lived inside the forest boundaries had to keep special rules. For instance, if he had a dog, he must cut off three claws from one of its front paws so that it could not run fast enough to chase the deer. He was usually allowed to collect small sticks for firewood, but woe betide him if he cut down the branch of an oak-tree! The king's foresters would be after him and he would be severely punished. If a dead deer was found in the woods and no one knew anything about it, all the people in the nearest village might be punished. The king's forest laws were harsh and grim.

At the end of his life William must have felt that he had succeeded pretty well in making both Normans and English obey him. Although there were still rebellious men, he had made the two peoples settle down together in the same country.

Since the Battle of Hastings a lot had happened. Now although William was always riding about the country, he could not have eyes everywhere. Remember that there were no good maps, no air-photographs, no radio or television, no telegraph or telephone. William was curious to know just what he had conquered in this land of England, what it was like, how rich it was, and what his Normans had been up to since he gave them their lands. He wanted, in fact, a picture of England.

So, about twenty years after he had conquered England, William called a great meeting of his council. Then he sent out messengers to all parts of England who were told to gather together the people from the villages in each district (or *hundred*, as it was called) and ask them many questions. They were to ask who used to own the land in the time of King Edward and who holds it now; how much land for ploughing and how many ox-teams to plough it; how many peasants there are; how many sheep, horses, cattle and pigs; how much woodland and pasture . . . and so on through a whole list of questions. The great barons, too, were asked for an account of their lands and this was checked against the account given by the villagers. So thoroughly was this done, that men said there was not a piece of land or an ox, cow or pig that was not written in the king's record. Many people grumbled and thought it was wrong of the king to be so inquisitive. Why should a king want to know about pigs and cows, they said? But William's orders always had to be obeyed and by and by clerks in different parts of the country were busy with hundreds of bits of *parchment*, putting together all the scraps of information they contained in one description. Finally these were all sent to Winchester, where the royal clerks copied them into what

48

we now call the Domesday Book. So King William got his picture of England, but before it was finished he was dead.

Here are three little pieces from William's Domesday Book. The first is the description of Godmanchester in Huntingdonshire:

In Godmanchester King Edward had 14 *hides*. There is land for 57 ploughs. There are two ploughs now on the king's *demesne*, and 80 *villeins* and 16 *bordars* have 24 ploughs. There is a priest and a church; 3 mills rendering 100 shillings; 160 acres of meadow; 50 acres of woodland for *pannage*. From the pasture come 20 shillings. From the meadows come 70 shillings. In the time of King Edward it was worth 40 pounds; now it is worth the same.

Secondly, Eynsford in Kent:

Ralph, son of Unspac, holds Eynsford from the archbishop. In the demesne there are 5 ploughs, and 29 villeins with 9 bordars have 15 ploughs. There are 2 churches and 9 slaves and 2 mills worth 43 shillings and 29 acres of meadow. Woodland for 20 pigs. In the time of King Edward it was worth 16 pounds; now 20. Of this manor Richard of Tonbridge holds woodland for 20 pigs and 1 mill and 1 fishpond.

Thirdly, Brooke in Norfolk:

Brooke was held by Earl Gyrth in the time of King Edward and King William gave it to the abbey of St. Edmund. There were then 33 villeins; now 38. Then as now 3 slaves. Now 3 ploughs on the demesne and 6 ploughs belonging to the men. Woodland for 30 pigs; 9 acres of meadow. Now 5 *rounceys*, 14 beasts, 40 pigs, 65 sheep, and 20 goats.

Remember that you can find the meaning of words printed like *this* in the Glossary at the end of this book. Can you decide which of these three places was the richest? And can you imagine what might have happened to Earl Gyrth?

Whatever people thought about William the Conqueror they never thought him lazy or feeble or weak-willed. You might expect that it would have been the Normans who praised him and the English who abused him when he died in 1087, but this was not so. You have already heard how one Norman blamed him severely for ordering the harrying of the north, and, on the other side, even the English had to admit that he had some good points. Like most men he did both good and bad deeds; when he died men remembered both. Here are the opinions of both sides—English and Norman. This was written by an Englishman, perhaps at Canterbury:

This King William was a very wise man and very powerful and more worshipful and stronger than any king before. He was gentle to the good men who loved God, and stern beyond all measure to those who disobeyed him. Also, he was very dignified: three times every year he wore his crown. At Easter he wore it at Winchester, at Whitsuntide at Westminster, and at Christmas at Gloucester, and then there were with him all the powerful men over all England, bishops, abbots, earls and knights. Also he was very stern and violent, so that no one dared do anything against his will. Amongst other things the good peace he made in this country is not to be forgotten. An honest man could travel over his kingdom without injury with his pockets full of gold and no one dared kill another. He protected the *harts* and boars, and loved the stags as much as if he were their father. These things we have written about him, both good and bad, that good men may imitate the good points and avoid the bad.

This was written by a monk in a monastery at Caen in Normandy :

This king was wiser than all the princes of his time. He never allowed himself to be stopped from carrying out a plan because it meant hard work and he was ever *undaunted* by danger. He was large and strong in body and tall in height. He never ate or drank too much and he hated drunkenness in all men. His voice was harsh, but he could easily persuade men to do what he wanted. He followed the Christian faith in which he had been brought up from childhood and whenever he could he attended Christian worship each morning and evening.

Here are some of the little designs embroidered in the borders of the Bayeux Tapestry.

HOW DO WE KNOW?

We are extremely lucky to have the whole exciting story of the Battle of Hastings told for us in a strip cartoon in needlework. These people could not take photographs or make films, but the women did not mind spending years with needle and thread, making pictures of the great stories they wanted to remember.

Who actually did the needlework? This is rather a puzzle and learned men still disagree about the answer. By looking closely at the pictures, two clues have been found. It has been noted that Odo, Bishop of Bayeux, is given a very important place in them; and also that some letters in the embroidered words are made in a special English way. So many people think that Odo ordered the tapestry to be made and that he got English women, who were famous then for their embroidery, to do it for him. Some people say that William the Conqueror's wife, Queen Matilda, made it with her ladies, but I think it is more likely to have been the English women. Someone who knew the whole story must have drawn the pictures for them to copy in stitches. I wonder if it made them sad to sew the story of the death of King Harold and the great English defeat. Perhaps they wept a little when they came to embroider Harold being struck by the arrow.

Can you picture them sitting in a row, perhaps, with part of the long strip across their knees? The embroidery was on coarse linen in strips about $19\frac{1}{2}$ inches wide which were sewn together in one long strip. This is now about 231 feet long, but some pictures at the end have been lost. The pictures are done in wool in eight colours (three shades of blue, two greens, red, yellow and grey), partly in outline or stem stitch and partly filled in in a way rather like our satin stitch. All sorts of interesting little things were embroidered in the borders—birds and animals, people hunting and ploughing, and so on. Some of these are drawn on the previous page. The main pictures have a great many figures in them. Do you know that in the whole tapestry there are 623 people, 202 horses and mules, 55 dogs, 505 other animals, 37 buildings, 41 ships, 49 trees?

hAROLD

In this drawing you can see the kind of stitches used to embroider the Bayeux Tapestry.

I wonder how long it took to do all these? Perhaps Odo ordered it when he was an important person in England, helping King William, his brother, to rule the country. Later, he was put in prison by William so I hope it was finished before then. Perhaps King William and Bishop Odo sat together while the long strip was unrolled in front of them—their nearest approach to a cinema show! Later it was taken to Odo's cathedral at Bayeux in Normandy and it is still in the town of Bayeux today.

CHRONICLES

Some of the monasteries liked to make their own history books. The Abbot would ask one monk to write a chronicle or history of all the important things which happened. Day after day he sat in the cloister or *scriptorium* working away. He would put down exciting events in the monastery or round about—a great flood or fire, the visit of a king or bishop, a plague among the sheep and so on—but he also wanted to record great happenings in the big world. He could not, of course, read newspapers to find out what was going on, so he had to rely on visitors, like the king's messengers who sometimes came galloping along the highway and stopped for the night in the monastery's guest-house. When he heard that a visitor had arrived the chronicler would hurry to the guest-house to get all the news he could. Sometimes a tired-out soldier came to stay and the chronicler would listen to his tales.

You can imagine that after the Battle of Hastings all the chroniclers were eager to get news of what was going on. So we can read today accounts of William and his Normans written soon after the Conquest. One famous chronicle was the Anglo-Saxon (or English) Chronicle. As you can guess, this was written by English monks and so tells what English men thought about William. On page 50 you will find a piece quoted from this chronicle.

Monks in Normandy also wrote about the Norman Conquest and so we can see it from their side too. On page 31 I have given a piece from a Norman chronicle and on page 51 another to show what a monk of Caen in Normandy thought of William.

54

Curiosity is often (though not always) a good thing. Because William the Conqueror was so inquisitive about his new kingdom, we have the Domesday Book, a wonderful description of the people and lands of England. On page 48 you will have read how William sent his men all through the counties to ask questions. The answers to those questions were finally gathered together and written in the two volumes, one bigger and one smaller, of the Domesday Book. For some time it was kept at Winchester and then brought to London. You can still see it today if you visit the Public Record Office in Chancery Lane.

For many centuries people looked in it to find out information about the land. Today we can still search it if we are curious to know what our town or village was like in the days of William the conqueror. But we need no longer go to London and puzzle over the curious lettering and the difficult Latin words of the original book, for most of it has been put into English and printed for us.

A piece of the original Domesday Book

If you go to your public library and ask for the Domesday description of your county, someone will probably be able to find it for you. If, however, you live in the extreme north of England or in Scotland or Wales, you will not find anything about your county in Domesday Book, for William's men did not go as far in their questioning. Can you guess why not?

A warning to you! Even when Domesday Book is put into English and clearly printed, it still has many difficult words in it and you may need help in understanding it. I have put down the rough meaning of a few words here, but you will probably have to ask your teacher to help you with others.

T.R.E.: in the time of Edward the King (Edward the Confessor).

T.R.W.: in the time of William the King.

demesne: land kept by the lord for himself.

villein: ordinary farm-worker, with his own house and land, but bound to work for his lord.

bordar: farm-worker with less land than the villein.

sokeman: small farmer, rather better off than the villein but still under a lord.

hide: about 120 acres of land.

virgate: about 30 acres of land.

THE WORDS EMBROIDERED ON THE BAYEUX TAPESTRY

These are in Latin and not always easy to read. Here you will find the Latin words and their English meaning for all the pictures in this book.

page

iv. HIC RESIDET HAROLD REX ANGLORUM Here sits Harold, King of the English.

1. ISTI MIRANT STELLA(M) These men wonder at the star.

3. HAROLD SACRAMENTUM FECIT WILLELMO DUCI Harold made an oath to Duke William.

5. HIC TRAHUNT NAVES AD MARE Here they drag the ships to the sea.

6. ISTI PORTANT ARMAS AD NAVES These men carry arms to the ships.

10. HIC WILLELM DUX . . . MARE . . . TRANSIVIT Here Duke William crossed over the sea.

10. ET VENIT AD PEVENESAE And came to Pevensey.

13. HIC MINISTRAVERUNT MINISTRI. HIC FECERUNT PRANDIUM Here the servants serve. Here they have dinner.

14. UT FODERETUR CASTELLUM AT HESTENGA (William) orders a castle to be dug at Hastings.

16. MILITES EXIERUNT DE HESTENGA The knights go out from Hastings.

16. ET VENERUNT . . . AD PRELIUM CONTRA HAROLDUM REGE(M) And advance to battle against Harold the King.

19. CECIDERUNT SIMUL ANGLI ET FRANCI English and French fell together.

19. HIC EST WILLELMUS DUX. Here is Duke William.

21. HAROLD REX INTERFECTUS EST King Harold was slain.

21. ET FUGA VERTERUNT ANGLI And the English fled.

THINGS TO DO

1. Cut out figures in wood or cardboard to represent Norman and English soldiers. Make a model of the Battle of Hastings using the descriptions and pictures in this book to help you.

2. Make your own "Bayeux Tapestry" of the Norman Conquest to go right round your classroom. You can use the pictures in this book as a guide, but you can add other scenes after the original tapestry stops, *e.g.* William marching to London, the harrying of the north, the fight against Hereward the Wake. Remember to draw your own pictures in the same style as the Bayeux Tapestry.

3. Study the Latin words on the Bayeux Tapestry and the English translations on the previous page. Can you discover the meaning of the following Latin words: STELLA, NAVES, ARMAS, MARE, CASTELLUM, MILITES? Can you think of English words we have made from these Latin ones?

4. Write the story of what happened in September and October 1066 as if told by one of Harold's soldiers.

5. Paint a picture of William's army besieging the island of Ely or write a poem about Hereward the Wake.

6. Write a letter from one of the Norman barons in England soon after the Conquest to his discontented wife in Normandy.

7. Write and act a scene between William and his barons in which the King is giving out land and telling the barons what services they have to do, while they take the oaths of homage and fealty.

8. Write a story about an English thegn who escapes abroad and has exciting adventures.

9. Find out if there is a Norman castle, cathedral or church near you. If so, visit it and make drawings. Look especially for thick, round pillars and round-headed arches and windows. What kinds of pattern did the Normans carve for decoration?

10. Make a model of a Norman castle.

11. Find out all you can about the Domesday description of your own town or village. Write and act a scene in which the Domesday enquirers come to your district and the villagers answer their questions.

12. Hold a class debate on whether William the Conqueror was a good or bad king.

13. Find out if there are any families still living in your county whose ancestors came over with William the Conqueror.

GLOSSARY

This is a list of special words. If the word you want to know is not here, look for it in your dictionary.

baron : a lord who was one of the King's chief men.
bordar : villager owning a very small piece of land.
causeway : a raised road built over marshy ground.
chattels : possessions (*e.g.* clothes, tools, furniture).
chain-mail : armour made of small metal rings linked together.
chronicle : history, generally written by monks.
demesne : land kept by the lord for himself.
fealty : a man's promise to be loyal to his lord.
ferocity : fierce cruelty.
feudal host : army of knights summoned by the King.
feudal service : the duty of fighting for the King when called upon.
fief : lands held by a baron or knight in return for service to the King.
hart : deer.
to harry : to destroy and lay waste.
hauberk : coat of chain-mail.
hide : about 120 acres of land.
homage : ceremony in which a knight receives land from his lord and promises service in return.
hundred : district smaller than a county.
javelin : short spear to be thrown in attack.
keep : strong stone fort, the centre of a Norman castle.
motte : mound on which the keep of a Norman castle was built.
muster : assembly of the army.
oath : solemn promise.
pannage : food for pigs in the woods, especially beech-nuts.
parchment : skin scraped smooth to use for writing.
peasant : villager who worked on the land.
prow : front of a ship.

rouncey : horse.

scriptorium : place in a monastery where writing was done.

sheriff : King's chief agent in each county.

sub-tenant : man holding land from a lord, not direct from the King.

tapestry : picture in needlework or woven into the cloth.

tenant-in-chief : lord holding land direct from the King.

thegn : an important man in the times before the Norman Conquest.

undaunted : unafraid.

vassal : man who had promised homage and fealty to a lord.

villein : villager who had his own house and land but was bound to work on his lord's farm.

witan : chief Council of the kings before the Norman Conquest.